UNDAR

42   9/23   £7

Undark

JOHN GLENDAY

*For Justine
with best wishes
[signature]
Edinburgh 2002*

PETERLOO POETS

First published in 1995
by Peterloo Poets
2 Kelly Gardens, Calstock, Cornwall PL18 9SA, U.K.

© 1995 by John Glenday

A catalogue record for this book is available
from the British Library

ISBN 1-871471-60-5

Printed in Great Britain by
Latimer Trend & Company Ltd, Plymouth

ACKNOWLEDGEMENTS are due to the editors of the following journals and anthologies in whose pages some of these poems, their translations or earlier versions first appeared:
Acteme; De Europese Lente (Belgium); *Event* (Canada); *Fine Madness* (USA); *Gairfish; Lines Review; Luceafârul* (Romania); *New Writing Scotland 6,7,8,10, 12* and *13; Northlight; Poetry Canada; Poetry Oxford; Secrets from the Orange Couch* (Canada); *Verse.*

'Over Vitebsk' was published in the 1st of May Poetry Prize Anthology.

'After Vesalius' won the 1994 X.E. Nathan Open Poetry Award.

The author gratefully acknowledges the assistance of the Scottish Arts Council and the Canada Council in the preparation of this book.

For Daniel and for Jack

My sons,
who raised me.

And in memory of Davy Brown,
died December 15th, 1993

"Y ya
cae sombra en el alma." (Vallejo)

Contents

AFTER VESALIUS

WAR PICTURES

UNDARK

The Leaving

for Jackie and Al

I light a candle
for your coming back,

brilliant and frail
in a darkening room.

Beautiful it is, and damned
not to last, only endure.

Almost as fragile
as darkness itself.

Famous Last Words

"... repito por el organo oral de tu silencio." Vallejo

I am a column of silence, resonating where it touches
on our world;
reluctant as silk drawn from flesh, or a harp
singing in its cage of wind.

My tongue is shaped by the sibilants of grass
upon air,
stone against thorn.

In my mouth
vowels age like seasons longing to become soil.

The trees with their arms laden.
The trees with empty hands.

I speak for the pause between waves,
for the night wind resting at the edges of itself
and the easy dissolution of clouds.

I speak for the snowfalls and the flecked granite,
for the mirrors clutching their people
of familiar smoke.

I speak for tomorrow's dust.

And I speak for my dark father, who floats face down
in the slack shadow-waters of memory, his mouth
rinsed clean of air.

I speak for want of silence.

Annunciation

And this was their appearance; they had the likeness of a man.
And every one had four faces, and every one had four wings.

We were discussing the construction of an angel's wings.
She'd found that old print of The Annunciation
where they arch above his head like an angry swan's
and cast down radiants of gold-coloured light on the hapless virgin.

She said feathers must mean angels were reptilian, essentially,
but if angels were fashioned on the lines of a god,
as we were, then surely they should be mammalian, and their wings,
                                        (if indeed
these are to be taken as more than mere bright conventions of
                                                artistry

like haloes, or the holy spirit hovering with a hawk's jizz)
their wings should be skin fixed on a framework of canted bone,
something like fruit bats or devils. *Quod erat demonstrandum,*
she said. *You know: qui mane oriebaris?*

She said that if angels had wings and if angels really were,
then in her opinion their wings would be like the wings of moths
which at rest lie open to display the stains of their stippled faith
like bark, or lichen, or wheatfields viewed from the air.

Angels hanker after light like moths, she said, but they hate the sun
and painlessly shed their talc. She said she imagined
if ever we touched them with our hands,
no matter how hard they tried, they would never quite fly again.

Nimbus

i.m. Davy Brown

In Tibetan Buddhism, the symbol for the mind's creative power
is not a light bulb, as in the Beano, but a cloud.
And I've heard that in Mexico they believe the dead
may speak from their graves for a short while after rain.
But Skye is nothing like Mexico.
They would never fall silent here.
Then perhaps it's true.

When I was seven, my father explained
how the dead converse through the telegraph wires
and it's only because we're stuck with being alive
that we can't understand what they say.
When I hugged the pole with him and listened,
their speech was thin and distant, but as heavenly as song.

A friend once described how he stood above Bernisdale
in a winter storm and watched the waves beat themselves
white against the gale, then surge up into the sky and disappear.
He said a blackface ewe went floundering past his door like
                                            tumbleweed.

I believe whatever has been done can only be translated, never
                                            undone.
That day, rain tasted salt at Invermoriston.

A Day at the Seaside

We're out in my father's boat and he's fishing.
He's fishing until the daylight goes.
It's the end of the season and I'm in the stern
to watch for the ebb that would pull us

out past the Buddon Light and the mouth of the river.
But I'm not watching the tide,
I'm watching him as he fishes, because I've never
seen him so focussed before — so engaged.

It's as if the fish had hooked him. Then just
as he makes his final cast, an oyster-catcher calls
far out across the water. Far out across
the water an oyster-catcher calls

just once, and then just once again, and then its silence calls.
The hurt lies not in the cross, but in the nails.

The Autumn Ghosts

There are no ghosts. Life
spirals into stillness round an armature
of dust. (You may have noticed

how a people of ragged smoke
drift through the corridors
of memory, beckoning silently?

These shapes are of no consequence —
they cast the frail skin
of the present tense

quite painlessly.) There are
no ghosts. Listen,
it was only the living that you heard

last night, as they called out
quietly in the oblique, dark rain.
Listen, they meant us no harm,

they will never return.
They were haunting the graves
of summers they would live again.

Edie's Room

for Mary Stewart

Just before dawn, I was woken
by the soft hush of the dead about their work.
It was cold in her room, so cold

I could see the half-bright cloud of my life
hung out in the air between the darkness
and the moon. I can't help but fall

for the dark each time it has to go.
Its death, like any other death, leads on
from mystery towards brighter mystery.

Dragging the Lake

for Daniel

Both hot fists brace themselves
against his chest, clutching
a hidden rope which strains down
through the sheets, into his dream.

Something has tethered him to something
he can't be rid of, or
there's some useless thing out there,
slick, unweildy — some dead

weight he just won't give up.
A burden heavier than his five
years is settling in the darkness,
snagged on pondweed and roots.

He'll never get it to budge.

When I stroke his head to settle him,
his fists spring open like a trap
and he cries out that shrill,
flat, desperate, battered-brain-stem cry
as a tiny figment of his life, or mine,
goes tumbling headlong through his dream
and just for the time it takes to drown,
comes true.

Inheritance

Forgive me, time,
the shell of my son,
who will break on the wheel of flowers,

though you half fill
my hand with your hand,
you will always be alone.

Forgive me, time,
who smile and gesture from
your tumbril of fishboxes and string;

whose trusting shadow
drifts through my shadow,
as spawn through a shrinking pool.

Forgive me, time,
who worship my inconstancies
on the fail shrine

of innocence.
I was your man-faced god,
but I built my own feet from clay.

Jacob's Story

*"The humane man loves mountains, and the love of stones
has the same meaning ..."* — Kong Chuan

To sleep with nothing but stone
between our heads and the stones which beat
at the centre of the Earth.

To sleep against silence,
wound in linen as cold as the moon,
the skull clean as a driven moon, and then suddenly

to dream of or understand that laborious commerce
of angels, who trade between worlds
their baggage of uselessly beating wings.

To sleep as the dead would sleep, (if only
we would let them sleep,)
with the head on its pillow of naked stone,

but imagining the heart.

Fire-Damp

And yet, I believe something
must sing in the heart.

I once read that when canaries
were taken underground

they would often sing back
towards what little light there was.

Penny's Dream

Broadway. Late 1920's.
Wall Street passes on stilts.
A man in a dark suit is pleading with a girl
to get on the tram with him,
but she insists on taking the train.
She'll be safe.

In the next compartment,
two dark-faced women, listening
from the corners of their ears,
plot her doom.
Tunnel lights whisk past
like burning soup plates.
The girl clutches her parcel more tightly.

A dusty heat wobbles towards
the indistinct horizon.
Dirt roads dribble away into the sky.
Now the taller of the two women
is strangling the girl in a ditch
and I can do nothing but scream at her to stop
then fall through the hollow quiet of the night,
breathlessly alert
and all my fingers throbbing.

Stories of the Wind

Why do you ask? There's no answer.
Only the half-lit gardens slanting
towards winter, and the railway
sidings and the listless sand dunes.
Oceans have foundered
on a clutch of marram.

Those clouds dismantling
themselves inside our mirror, listen,
they whisper in their hopeless majesty:
Why don't you ask?

There's no answer.

Pet

In the fungussy
shadows
of its varnished hutch

with
stale food / damp straw / shit
stuccoing matted fur,

Love
feebly knocks the hind leg
that is not tied down with wire

against
the strongest angles
of my shirt

Preserve Me More Perfectly

Preserve me more perfectly
memory of another,
freed of this distant

flesh, this withering blood.
Hold on to me more
carefully than I hold you,

who drift from
my sleeping hands
as threadbare as smoke.

Preserve me
as the moon preserves
the shadow of its influence

in the chambers of a whitened shell,
where a fist sized ocean trembles
and your own blood calls.

The Snow Queen

"'It seems to me as if someone were behind us," said Gerda ...
... "These are only Dreams!" said the Raven'

Love is not the young couple on the rooftop,
nor is it the roses which spoke,
nor the clever raven,
nor the good princess and her good prince asleep in their separate
                                         beds,
nor the murderous robber-wife,
nor the robber-maid tugging a frightened girl into her bed,
nor is love her knife pressed to the girl's ribs,
nor even the talking deer which carried the girl away,
nor is it the old Lapland woman who scratched a few words
on a flank of dried stock-fish,
nor Spitzbergen,
nor that long journey barefoot through the world,
nor Kay, black with cold,
nor those healing tears unkindness made.

And love is not the heart,
nor is it the frozen heart,
nor even the heart unfrozen.

Love
is that splinter of mirrored glass, and a wound of the same shape
as that splinter of glass
and a cracked reflection that seems larger than the larger world.

25

Mitra Mitra

The sea moves through our sleep
from room to room.
The curtains sway to the slush
of its punctured heart.

The sea's insistent, confidential
breath has rinsed away all other sounds.
What were we saying to one another?
Why did we come together

in the first place? I didn't ask
to drown, but I have drowned.
No one will find the shell
in which our love resounds.

Portage

We carry the dead in our hands.
There is no other way.

The dead are not carried in our memories. They died
in another age, long before this moment.
We shape them from the wounds
they left on the inanimate,
ourselves, as falling water
will turn stone into a bowl.

There is no room in our hearts
for the dead, though we often imagine that there is,
or wish it to be so,
to preserve them in our warmth,
our sweet darkness, where their fists
might beat at the soft contours of our love.
And though we might like to think
that they would call out to us, they could never do so,
being there. They would never dare to speak,
lest their mouths, our names, fill
quietly with blood.

We carry the dead in our hands
as we might carry water — with a careful,
reverential tread.
There is no other way.

How easily, how easily their faces spill.

The Interiors of Former Cars

Sometimes I find myself trying to visualise the dashboard layouts of all the cars I have ever owned — everything from that hairsprung Citroen to the thirsty sea-blue Chevrolet which died in its sleep.

It's always as dark inside them then as it is here now. I hunt around with my feet for pedals, fumble for the ignition switch and gears, trying to figure out again how it was I once made them work.

For some reason it's the steering wheel which comes back most clearly every time. I don't know why — perhaps because I held on to it more.

It seems to me I can remember the roads I drove down better than those cars, better even than the people I was with, though they were the more constant, usually. Why should that be?

Those cars settle on their perished tyres in dust-grey lockups, like memories that will no longer work for us. They'll always be unreliable. And no matter the useless oil-stained hours we might spend tinkering with them, they'll never go.

Concerning the Atoms of the Soul

Someone explained once how the pieces of what we are
fall downwards at the same rate
as the Universe.
The atoms of us, falling towards the centre

of whatever everything is. And we don't see it.
We only sense their slight drag in the lifting hand.
That's what weight is, that communal process of falling.
Furthermore, those atoms carry hooks, like burrs,

hooks catching like hooks, like clinging to like,
that's what keeps us from becoming something else,
and why in early love, we sometimes
feel the tug of the heart snagging on another's heart.

Only the atoms of the soul are perfect spheres
with no means of holding on to the world
or perhaps no need for holding on,
and so they fall through our lives catching

against nothing, like perfect rain,
and in the end, he wrote, mix in that common well of light
at the centre of whatever the suspected
centre is, or might have been.

Last Night it Rained

"My heart beats in my skull" — Wolf Biermann

Last night when it rained it rained ink.
It rained so hard the moon turned blue
and the pale blue stars sank
through a permanent black sky.

It rained and the ink lay in pools everywhere.
This morning the early commuters
trailed out their autobiographies
in the neglected language of the sole.

Some stumbled backwards, reading
themselves, while others tossed their shoes
aside and marvelled at the Aztec
numerals of their toes. We all choose,

because we all have somewhere to go
and we get there sooner if we learn
to watch where we've been. Nostalgia is a light to look forward to.
The head turns back and reads. The heart walks on.

The Button Accordionist

for Ellis Armstrong

What I would really like is to be able to type
the words with these fingers and punctuate with these.
Syllables and silences, pauses and sentences.

Perhaps a fresh book might open
with each breath of the hands, and instead of ink
I'd use plush, velvety pleats to hold the sense secure.
No matter how widely the pages fanned
not a word would be lost.

And I wish I could forge a rich and cursive music
with my pen — a music that couldn't help but rhyme,
that always and never meant,
that sang what it didn't quite sing.

Colours

Memory is blue. Yes,
blue as cracked porcelain or
jazz music.

The faces in memory are brown
or sometimes grey, due
to the film of tarnished

love which often overlies
the frame. (This gently rusts
to a rich mahogany. Thereafter,

completely and quite beautifully, black.)
Love, as you might have guessed, is red,
thanks to the mesh of small veins

webbing the lid's cup. The eye
is most often closed, for love also
loves to be blind, or at best myopic.

Oh and of course anger
and jealousy are both black — all
colours gelling together.

But memory,
memory is always blue,
more and more blue

the further back we gaze.
And isn't it lovely,
like this, casually reviewing

the perspectives of forever,
although we never seem to be quite
sure if that should be

a field
a cloud
a face?

Concerning Shadows

We all cast shadows,
even the sun, perhaps.
Only shadows have no shadows.
Shadows cast us.

Normally the shadow lies prone —
its grave is the sunlight —
but sometimes we come upon it
leaning against a wall
with its limbs broken.

There are no shadows inside shadows.
Shadows are barren,
though we may contain shadows
as shadows may contain us.

Our shadows are no paler in the moonlight,
only we are.

Nothing can injure shadows,
but when floated on water
even a feather will crack them.

It's only when we lie down that our shadows fit.

Shadows are as gentle
and momentary as snow.
They can't thrive without light,
but light also withers them.
In this respect, they resemble people.

Be careful:
always keep yourself between
your shadow and the sun.

At Barry Mill

I wish I could be chaff. I like chaff best of all.
Closer to dust than bread,
chaff drifts downwind of the beaten seed
and as with the soul — our heart's chaff — sails

for a moment through its banister of light.
Deep in the workings of the heart stone turns on stone
and those stones are milled by the flow of the constant grain.
But I'll settle for chaff. I hanker after things that have no weight.

A Nest of Boxes

"This is Natures nest of Boxes; The Heavens contain the Earth, the Earth, Cities, Citie.
Men. And all these are Concentrique; the common center to them all, is decay, ruine,"
— John Donne: Devotions

The heavens contain the earth,
and in the heart
of the earth beats

the ocean, and in the warm
hollows of the ocean
a child dreams,

and at the very core
of his dream
the heavens turn

on the axis
of a further dream
— dreaming that they lie

distant from the world;
dreaming how they will never
need to fall.

The Loom

What held him suspended, grey fathoms
above sleep?

Not the silent wife beside him,
two decades into strangeness,

nor the sullen youth kicking
dust into moonlight,

nor the familiar, evaporating dream
of oars threshing corn in a kingdom

without sea.
Only a hank of darkness on the untouched

loom, weaving a shroud
which would not be undone.

On the Legend of Euridice

Looking back on it,
he might have caught a twist
of shadow curled against a stone,
or sensed that slap of air, the carcass
of her voice; and darkness
oozing from her mouth like oil.

Or worse, much worse than that,
imagine this:
tormented by the plodding silence more than love,
(her mouth stopped with the dung of myth)
he turns back to discover the woman
also turning back.

She gazes longingly into the stillness
he has fouled, that lightless Eden he calls Hell.
Her name, his tuneful promises, rush
towards vacuum. A swirl of momentary fragrance.
Unearthly flowers wilting
at the same speed as her hand.

Nettles

Between the hearthstone
and the machair,

between the prefabs
and the factory,

between the bleachfields
and the river,

between the rhubarb
and the bicycle,

we are struck down
and we rise up again.

No one dares touch us.
No one will honour us.

We are our own gods.

Alba

Some say she looks like an old witch,
a dark caillich with a cat's-tail of islands for hair.
Brine sluices the words from her cracked lips.
I say no. I say she's as fresh as these flakes
of schist and quartzite I gathered yesterday.

Some say she's barren: *"Look how they scoured*
her bairns from her womb with a dab of wool," they say,
"and them scarce halfways down the road to birth.
The four airts buried them.
Their cries will will circle the earth like little storms."
I say no. I say she's poor but whole and strong
and I've heard her children sing out in our half dark street,
barely a whisper before night.

Some say she's bad news, a temptress, a whistler on ships,
that the man who sleeps with her will wake one morning
at dusk on a hillside under the brisk rain, his pockets weighted with
                                                          sand.
I say no. I say, look at me: I've slept with her all the nights of my
                                                          life
and still each morning when I wake I find her tongue in my mouth.

Pale Flower

*In 1774 the first anatomical dissection of a human body ever carried out in Japan was
performed using Dutch textbooks upon the body of the famous Geisha, Pale Flower.*

A longitudinal incision
through the skull reveals
a brain soft but resiliant;

the tongue well anchored in its —
page forty-three — cartilaginous bed.
Trachea clear of speech.

That fist-sized mash of dark grain
in the gut would be her last meal, stained
with altered blood.

Good musculature abdominally,
though paler than the illustration.
Pale Flower. Bloodlessly beautiful.

Let us fold back these petals.
Note how the pistil remains
lush, even beyond death.

Such is the vessel she was.
See here, where that slack root,
her obedience,

adheres; the gourd hangs
moist, but sterile.
That's enough. Returning to the head,

these arteries which channel
through the neck sustained her intellect.
More necessary still,

this fine mesh, here and here, spread
strands of blood, like saffron, through her cheeks,
whenever it was right, or so desired.

Undark

And so they come back, those girls who painted
the watch dials luminous and died.

They come back and their hands glow and their lips
and hair and their footprints gleam in the past like alien snow.

It was as if what shone in them once had broken free
and burned through the cotton of their lives.

And I want to know this: how they came to believe
that something so beautiful could ever have turned out right,

but though they open their mouths to answer me,
all I can hear is light.

The Ngong Peony

'We have not succeeded in growing peonies in Africa,' he said, 'and shall not do so till we manage to make an imported bulb flower here, and can take the seed from that flower. This is how we got delphinium into the colony ...'

This is the truth:
Blixen brought with her into Africa
the *Duchesse de Nemours*,
a 'rich and noble' peony which bloomed
once from a solitary head,
magically huge and pale.

The light seemed to condense around its globe
which rose through a ground
of dark, lush, curvilinear leaves.
It thrived as none other had before,
nor ever would again, in all that continent.

She picked it, of course,
and within four days
it had laid its brilliance on her carpet,
shell by shell.

But it sang in those days,
it sang as the cicada sings
when it draws out the brief chord of its joy,
burnishing the daylight from itself: that carapace,
these words, this overwhelming dusk.

Estuarine

Have you ever noticed how the sound of the sea and the sound of
                                                    the wind
are so remarkably alike, so consonant in the darkness, breathing in
                                                    harmony,
how the one stirs up the other,
and they always seem to die in each other's arms?

You've forgotten for a moment how disparate these elements are,
that may be the reason for their embrace, as if they knew they
                                                    would always
stay this far apart — as distant as hand is from glove, mo matter the
                                                    season,
no matter how close together they might lie, no matter the weather.
I sometimes wonder if that's why they seem to sing the way they
                                                    do.

AFTER VESALIUS

The Empire of Lights

After Magritte: L'Empire des Lumieres 1954

The past is the antithesis of burglary. Imagine
a house in darkness. Or to be more precise,
imagine darkness in a house. Something akin

to that Magritte where the light is held
at tree's length by a clutch of tungsten bulbs.
The looming woods proofed with shadow thicker than tar.

In the House of the Past we move backwards
from room to room, forever closing doors
on ourselves, always closing doors.

In each room, we leave some of those little trinkets
we love most, that the house is stealing from us.
Because we cherish them, we abandon them

to the furniture of strangers. Whenever we go
the doors swing shut behind us without a sound,
and the dust drifts up into the ceiling like smoke.

Oh there is so much we would love to hold on to,
but so little room. If only we could come back,
if only we could come back in the morning,

things would be so much better. But on we must go,
creeping backwards through silent bedrooms,
closing doors quietly for fear of waking ourselves.

Emptying our pockets, emptying our hands. Heavy
with emptiness, we crouch down at last in the lee
of a shattered window, where we dream of those

ancient burdens, long resolved. And the fragments
of glass fidget like broken insects on the rug,
eager to heal where our fists will gently touch.

Son of Man

after Magritte: Le Fils de L'homme

There are times
when in the most unhindered light
we can discern shadows

cast by something less
than visible. Imprints or absences
our bodies, somehow, lie beyond.

There are times when history
flows through us
like a trembling music,

as though, invested
with the sea, we had ourselves
become an instrument.

And there are times
when all our weaknesses hang
ripening between us

and ourselves. Those ancient,
unencompassed frailties we could not look
beyond, nor hide behind.

The Evening Dress

After Magritte: La Robe du Soir

Eventually, she will go back
to the sea. For now,
a whisper of its depth in the marram grass.
Further inland, a house abandoned
since the summer — windows out—
the front hall primed with sand.
She doesn't seem to care.
Perhaps she smiles.

I can imagine she might smile — her skin
clothed in a fine, close weave
of borrowed light — nothing beyond.
Brine crystallizing on the downsweep of her breasts,
her sex a folded sprig.

How alien she looks, going away,
with the sum of things I thought I understood
inhumed in light
and the buried, terribly revealed.

Behind her, me, the dark side
of the moon, her life shifting
like dunes, the smoky gloss of hair
falling as far as always, tangled
against her nakedness,
the shadow of a person
smaller than I ever thought I'd be.

The Song of the Violet

After Magritte: Le Chant de la Violette 1951

There is a special dust which gathers in the heart
on winter afternoons: the last of the daylight
thins to a distant thrum, whatever of myself I saw
as false suddenly becomes unknown, luminous or true.
But the moment dies, it burns through the lining
of the soul like joy and its passing,

its passing puts the death and life in me.
If we were free once, we were free, and being free,
traded that freedom for this,
because we wanted more — more than a choice,
more than mere absence of despair —
the brilliance and the savagery of one squandered hour.

The Woman Who Bathed
Between Light and Darkness

After Magritte: Baigneuse du clair au sombre 1935

The Ocean is rectangular.
It folds and folds
within the confines of its frame —
my listening hand.

Beyond closed eyes
a consummate darkness breathes.
The circumference of the Earth,
but turning the other way.

Both sing inside me, singing inside them.

This much I love, or comprehend.

Over Vitebsk

After Chagall

Grandfather came home early from a war
that had never been. I remember he looked
quite regimental in his winter coat

and battered postman's cap, as he dangled
like gathered smoke between the rooftops
and the sky. I was roused by the rap

of his white stick on our slates. Behind me
a voice hissed: *"He's calling
our names, I think. Listen!"*

And I think he was: softly at first, but quite
insistently. The moon of his face bleached
green by the chlorine gas and cold.

Then suddenly nothing seemed straight
any more. Dawn spiralled in flames.
Snow curved through the runnel of our street.

The Market Square (no longer square)
had gently liquefied into a milky lens.
Even the steeple where he moored himself

was yawing crazily above its arc of little graves.
He called out again with greater urgency,
and not just our names, but something like:

... something *'man'* and then *'land'* and then something
'gone' ... Though we craned in the yard with our ears
cupped, we still couldn't make him out.

The youngsters lobbed rocks and insults
as he raved: "Where's your rifle, Grandad?"
"Show us a skull!"

Gobs of spittle began to drench us — they reeked
of a thin despair — so we wafted our caps and bonnets,
winnowed his chaff away.

"Peace at last, praise God." whispered Nana,
crossing herself again, as the last few strands
of his message darkened the earth, like rain.

Attitudes of Animals in Motion

after Eadweard Muybridge

I have exposed a stillness, beating
in the heart of things — motion's diastole.

When I dissected the path from a to b
I demonstrated to the world that life is no smooth progression
through the flux, but rather fractions
of utter rest, stacked to infinity.
How then, do we ever arrive?

The cripple and the palomino and the nude
advancing with a bayonet
freeze to a statuesque inertia.
Each muscle, contoured by its ply of forces
hints at an obdurate vitality
snuffed in the moment's hand.

But there's more life in this portrait
of my late wife (whom I loved
despite her ways) than all those
Palo Alto trotters breaking strings.
(Their cardboard hooves still race
around a tin loop in a cupboard somewhere.
Let them run.)

Beside her head, a severed branch
droops with abundances of pear.
Note how her lids droop likewise
in the heat of gestating illness.
One hand rests on her abdomen, attractively

deformed by the larval mass
of 'Little Harry' — Flora's only son.

I made an orphan once.

We, being we, wherever on the earth
we go, break strings, which momently
transfix our lives, then leave us
dispossessed and free.

A Panoramic View of San Francisco

after the photographs by Eadweard Muybridge

Sepia suits clapboard well.
It varnishes the houses with a period air,
their dusty stoops and cedar
shingles gleaming wearily. We can almost smell

the pitch and resin. Street after vacant street
banks down towards the water. Scoured paths
and pavements of compacted mud craze
in the morning heat.

A panoramic view of San Francisco.
He laid out the surrounding precincts
frame by frame, like freshly chloroformed insects.
But his plates were slow.

Even at the widest aperture
exposure times were what —
seconds at least? Enough to let
things that were quick enough rub through

into transparency. Hundreds of passers-by
were turned to a threadbare gauze
when they crossed between his camera and the haze
of distant light. Perhaps the currency

of immortality is stasis
rather than enduring power,
genius or evil. Once, someone wrote, means never.
Most of us falter simply through living once.

Notice that packhorse, tethered by
the neck to history, its head fudged
into anonymity where it ducked
to dislodge a fly.

That half-presence shows how bodies sometimes turn
to dust because they move.
Scratch love, shadows, ignorance or the grave,
it's what we see which makes us blind.

After Vesalius

"Useless ... useless ... " — John Wilkes Booth

Among the illustrations in Vesalius' *De Humani Corporis Fabrica*
I saw a dead man lift up in wonder his marvellous, flayed hands.
Fibres of raw muscle hung from both wrists, as heavy as purses
                                        filled with blood.
Behind him fields ripened slowly, little weathers grew,
and the spires of his village rose between chocolate-box hills.

Although we also must seem dead, in a manner of speaking,
(our breadth of speech, depth of thought, length of custom)
we will stand rooted to this country which has gouged us crotch to
                                         tongue,
with all those inner workings we had hoped would let us move
resected and laid bare. Such is the case in agony or love.

WAR PICTURES

Leaving Afghanistan

(found poem from New York Times, January 8th 1989)

Tass reported that Lieut. General Boris Gromov, the commander of Soviet Forces in Afghanistan, would be the last Soviet soldier to leave the country, crossing the border at the Soviet town of Termez at 10.00am on February 15th.

'He will cross without looking back,' it said.
'Then he will stop and make a speech,
but only to himself.

It will last one minute and seven seconds.

It will not be written down, or listened to ...'

War Pictures

Five icons and a photograph.
In memoriam John Goodfellow Glenday: 1913-1988

1. CRETE 1941

I was Nobody with a rifle
when the paratroopers came.
A Nobody with a rifle
I couldn't fire, guarding
a Nothing I wouldn't remember,
in a Nowhere I'd never forget.

The sergeant sent me up a rotten ladder
to the open, whitewashed roof:
"Have a quick shufti at what's going on."
I crouched by the cistern,
clutching my rifle like
an awkward branch, hoping
to god no one would notice me.

Stukas with folded wings
were falling like gannets
on the road to Maleme.
A vague, sporadic gunfire fumbled
closer, smacking grey
cups in the walls below me.

The ladder having been removed
by a panicking lieutenant,
there was nowhere I could run,
so I threw myself down on the blank page
of the roof, praying for all I was,
all I might never be.
My loosened tin hat dotting
the i of me.

2. FREIGHT

We spent a week in cattle trucks,
creeping from Greece to the Sudetenland.
The tougher prisoners shoved
their way to the plum spots
by the ventilators, but
the doors stayed locked four days.
We had no choice but to force
our faeces through those nose-high grilles.

Old Harper laughed at that as
he sucked on his empty pipe:
*"Remember, son, the strong aye
claim the cleaner air,
but they smell of shite ..."*

3. JOCKEYS. SUDETENLAND 1941

Jolted awake in
the perpetual twilight
of nowhere, we were moths
pulled to the dusty,
slatted sunlight
and the muffled laughter.

Round a meadow by the sidings
jockeys in pressed
silk paraded their
never decreasing circles.

4. Dead Meat. Stalag XIIIB

A double charm
against escape:
Herr Knappek

made us watch
as the camp guards
bayonetted

our tins
of Red Cross
bully beef.

5. Window

Long after the contrails
of the bombers had drifted
back to immaculate blue,
tatters of silver paper
tumbled from the sky.

Guards looked at prisoners,
prisoners looked at guards.
Some blamed it on the Russians,
others waited for the world to end.

One fellow, knocking
the mud from his boots
against a wall, said
perhaps it was only
God in his little firmament
weeping at the products
of our squandered freedom.

6. BEACH HALL, MONIFIETH. 1946

Doomed by those low,
octobering clouds of June,
another half-cocked venture fails.

But he poses boldly enough
for the camera, thrusting
two ice cream cones no one will buy
at two smiling children.
He looks at neither.

Their faces are folded in shadow,
but at the centre of it all
he holds out before him
those two ice creams
like twin lamps of ignorance
and his pale future gleams.

Whitman's War

1. DRIVING CATTLE THROUGH WASHINGTON

They would pass by in dust,
often towards nightfall. Quite orderly
for the most part,

hardly glancing to either side.
The fearful or the obstinate
might break ranks for a moment,

tossing their great heads back, eyes
white and wild. The outriders —
their file-closers — easily

driving them back. They would pass
slowly down the wide avenues
and out of sight.

Whitman noted the melodic call of the drovers:
"... a wild, pensive hoot, quite musical,
... something between a pigeon and an owl."

He would watch from a distance
as the great regiments hushed
and grew smaller,

perhaps a thousand or more,
moving south. He would stand on the stoop
in his slouch hat

long after they had gone,
shielding his eyes in case the dust
should make them cry.

2. VISITING THE ARMORY SQUARE HOSPITAL

He drifts from cot to cot,
through the sweet, warm scent
of lamplight and fever, distributing
comforts to the men
that ball and canister
knocked down.

If they cannot sleep
he writes their letters for them:

"Dear Sis,
make it so Mama never comes. Send
rice pudding. Some of her pickles."

For a big man he is soft, soft
and strangely kind. Before he leaves,
he will lay by each bed some splinters
of horehound candy, a clutch of cents,
or a modest notebook for their words.

Here's that Michigan farm boy,
poor'n skim piss, the butt
of his left leg
moist and blackening,
who reaches out carefully
within the confines of his pain to leaf
through his little book, bound
in a fetching, marbled blue,
and all its pages blank.

3. Our Wonderful Inventions

The Patent Office in Washington was used as a temporary hospital during the early years of the war.

Yellowing dust slants
through the cluttered light
and settles against the oak framed cabinets
that hold our wonderful inventions:
industrial machinery in miniature,
abstruse devices, gifts
from foreign potentates —
all numbered, labelled and unused.
The terminal moraine of genius,
to be preserved at all costs.

For want of space
they laid us between the glass cases,
we hopeless cases.
The dying by the steam accordian,
the fancy roller skates beside the amputees.
And we lay there thinking to ourselves:

*What a lot of new ideas there seem to be
these days! Why there's hardly room enough
to house them all, and men besides.*

And we were ordinary men
who stood out from the ranks
just once — it was our only fault.
Neither the first nor best,
we withered early. Friend,
note down our names.

4. ARTILLERY HORSES UNDER FIRE

That slap the minie balls make when they strike
sickens the heart. Sounds just like pebbles
smacking into mud.

Mostly they fall straight off, then struggle
up again, shivering and stiff, but strangely
quiet till the next round comes.

Some simply twitch their flanks or slash
their tails across the wound, staring ahead.
You'd think it was a blowfly at them,

nothing more. I remember at Cold Harbor we watched
as the last from a team of six stood firm
in harness with five bullets in her side.

She toppled only when the sixth ball sheared
through bone. Not one was spooked, nor ran;
but then, the living were left limbered

to the dead. We could hear the rebels cheer
as horse after horse dropped through its traces,
kicking the caisson sides.

They hardly make no sound — that's what I hate.
Die as they must, God damn them.
I don't know. Some beasts act more like men.

Blind

I was thinking of what you said
and it isn't true. Who can say what will come
and what will come to nothing?

You seemed so far away.
The moon had long set, but something distant and cold
shone through the half-open window

and the form that lay beside me in the bed
seemed less than an absence smoothed into the dark.
That night, I held you not for warmth or pardon, but for light.

Remember that blind man
who once passed us in the street?
How he touched his stick gently

against the world — just confirming the world
still travelled with him — then strode on as if something
that was not darkness lay ahead?